NATIONAL GEOGRAPI

T0069698

My Family Keeps Fit

David Tunkin

My family is active.
We like to keep fit.

My mom likes to walk.
She walks to work.
Walking helps keep her fit.

My **dad** likes to jog.
He jogs around the park.
Jogging helps keep him fit.

adidas

My brother likes to shoot baskets. He shoots baskets at the park. Shooting baskets helps keep him fit.

DO NOT
HOLD ONTO RING

My sister likes to swim.
She swims at the swimming pool.
Swimming helps keep her fit.

SURFER
FUN!

I like to ride my bike.
I ride my bike on the bike path.
Riding my bike helps keep me fit.
How do you keep fit?